To

....

From

....

God Tenderly Comforts You

A PROMISE JOURNAL

© 2009 Ellie Claire Gift & Paper Corp.
www.ellieclaire.com

Compiled by Joanie Garborg
Designed by Lisa & Jeff Franke

Scripture references are from the following sources: The Holy Bible, King James Version (KJV). The
New King James Version (NKJV). Copyright © 1982 by Thomas Nelson, Inc. Used by permission.
The Holy Bible, English Standard Version® (ESV), copyright © 2001 by Crossway Bibles, a publishing
ministry of Good News Publishers. Used by permission. The New American Standard Bible® (NASB),
Copyright © 1960, 1962, 1963, 1968, 1971, 1972, 1973, 1975, 1977, 1995 by The Lockman Foundation.
Used by permission. The Holy Bible, New International Version®, NIV® Copyright © 1973, 1978,
1984 by International Bible Society. Used by permission of Zondervan. The Holy Bible, New Living
Translation (NLT), copyright 1996, 2004. Used by permission of Tyndale House Publishers, Inc.,
Wheaton, Illinois. The Message. Copyright © 1993, 1994, 1995, 1996, 2000, 2001, 2002. Used by
permission of NavPress, Colorado Springs, CO. The Living Bible (TLB) © 1971. Used by permission
of Tyndale House Publishers, Inc., Wheaton, Illinois 60189. All rights reserved.

ISBN 978-1-935416-11-1

Printed in China

God Tenderly Comforts You

A PROMISE JOURNAL

Ellie Claire
gift & paper expressions

...inspired by life

The God of All Comfort

We may ask, "Why does God bring thunderclouds
and disasters when we want green pastures and still waters?"
Bit by bit, we find behind the clouds, the Father's feet;
behind the lightning, an abiding day that has no night;
behind the thunder, a still small voice
that comforts with a comfort that is unspeakable.

OSWALD CHAMBERS

Regardless of the need, God comforts.
He is the God of all comfort!
That's His specialty.

CHARLES R. SWINDOLL

God walks with us.... He scoops us up in His arms
or simply sits with us in silent strength
until we cannot avoid the awesome recognition
that yes, even now, He is here.

GLORIA GAITHER

_he Lord is near to the brokenhearted and
saves those who are crushed in spirit._

PSALM 34:18 NASB

Comforted by God

Blessed be the God and Father of our Lord Jesus Christ,
the Father of mercies and God of all comfort,
who comforts us in all our affliction
so that we will be able to comfort
those who are in any affliction
with the comfort with which we ourselves
are comforted by God.

2 CORINTHIANS 1:3–4 KJV

May our Lord Jesus Christ himself and God our Father,
who loved us and by his grace gave us eternal
comfort and a wonderful hope, comfort you and
strengthen you in every good thing you do and say.

2 THESSALONIANS 2:16–17 NLT

I, even I, am he who comforts you.

ISAIAH 51:12 NIV

....

....

....

....

....

....

....

....

....

....

....

....

....

....

....

....

....

Only God can truly comfort; He comes alongside us and shows us how deeply and tenderly He feels for us in our sorrow.

Lift Up Your Eyes

It should fill us with joy that infinite wisdom guides the affairs of the world...that infinite wisdom directs every event, brings order out of confusion, and light out of darkness, and to those who love God, causes all things, whatever be their present aspect and apparent tendency, to work together for good.

J. L. DAGG

I lift up mine eyes to the quiet hills,
and my heart to the Father's throne;
in all my ways, to the end of days,
the Lord will preserve His own.

TIMOTHY DUDLEY-SMITH

Faith is to believe what we do not see; and the reward of this faith is to see what we believe.

AUGUSTINE

*I lift my eyes to you, O God, enthroned in heaven.
We keep looking to the LORD our God for his mercy.*

PSALM 123:1–2 NLT

God Understands

He heals the brokenhearted and bandages their wounds.
He counts the stars and calls them all by name.
How great is our Lord! His power is absolute!
His understanding is beyond comprehension!…
No, the LORD's delight is in those who fear him,
those who put their hope in his unfailing love.

PSALM 147:3–5, 11 NLT

Trust in the LORD with all thine heart; and lean
not unto thine own understanding. In all thy ways
acknowledge him, and he shall direct thy paths.

PROVERBS 3:5–6 KJV

Our help is in the name of the LORD,
who made heaven and earth.

PSALM 124:8 KJV

Everything God does is love—even when we do not understand Him.

BASILEA SCHLINK

Place of Rest

Breathe, O breathe Thy loving Spirit
into every troubled breast;
let us all in Thee inherit,
let us find Thy promised rest.

CHARLES WESLEY

Trust Him when dark doubts assail thee
Trust Him when thy strength is small,
Trust Him when to simply trust Him
Seems the hardest thing of all.

Trust Him, He is ever faithful;
Trust Him, for His will is best;
Trust Him, for the Heart of Jesus,
Is the only place of rest.

*In returning and rest shall ye be saved; in quietness
and in confidence shall be your strength.*

Isaiah 30:15 KJV

God's Guidance

To You, O LORD, I lift up my soul.
O my God, in You I trust, do not let me be ashamed;
do not let my enemies exult over me.
Indeed, none of those who wait for You will be ashamed....
Make me know Your ways, O LORD; teach me Your paths.
Lead me in Your truth and teach me,
for You are the God of my salvation;
for You I wait all the day.
Remember, O LORD,
Your compassion and Your lovingkindnesses,
for they have been from of old.

PSALM 25:1–6 NASB

You guide me with your counsel,
leading me to a glorious destiny.

PSALM 73:24 NLT

He stilled the storm to a whisper;
the waves of the sea were hushed.
They were glad when it grew calm,
and he guided them to their desired haven.

PSALM 107:29–30 NIV

The Lord is able to guide. The promises cover every imaginable situation....
Take the hand He stretches out.

ELISABETH ELLIOT

The Goodness of God

The goodness of God is infinitely more wonderful
than we will ever be able to comprehend.

A. W. TOZER

All that is good, all that is true, all that is beautiful,
all that is beneficent, be it great or small,
be it perfect or fragmentary,
natural as well as supernatural,
moral as well as material, comes from God.

JOHN HENRY NEWMAN

We walk without fear, full of hope and courage
and strength to do His will,
waiting for the endless good which He is always giving
as fast as He can get us able to take it in.

GEORGE MACDONALD

Open your mouth and taste, open your eyes and see—how good God is.
Blessed are you who run to him. Worship God if you want the best;
worship opens doors to all his goodness.

PSALM 34:8–9 THE MESSAGE

God's Thoughts

Your thoughts—how rare, how beautiful! God, I'll never
comprehend them! I couldn't even begin to
count them—any more than I could count the sand of
the sea. Oh, let me rise in the morning and live always with you!

PSALM 139:17–18 THE MESSAGE

The counsel of the LORD stands forever,
the plans of his heart to all generations.

PSALM 33:11 NKJV

How great are your works, O LORD,
how profound your thoughts!

PSALM 92:5 NIV

"My thoughts are nothing like your thoughts," says the LORD.
"And my ways are far beyond anything you could imagine.
For just as the heavens are higher than the earth,
so my ways are higher than your ways
and my thoughts higher than your thoughts."

ISAIAH 55:8–9 NLT

Just when we least expect it, He intrudes into our neat and tidy notions about who He is and how He works.

JONI EARECKSON TADA

Mighty to Keep

God is adequate as our keeper....
Your faith will not fail
while God sustains it;
you are not strong enough to fall away
while God is resolved to hold you.

J. I. PACKER

God, who is our dwelling place, is also our fortress.
It can only mean one thing, and that is,
that if we will but live in our dwelling place,
we shall be perfectly safe and secure from every assault.

HANNAH WHITALL SMITH

God of the years that lie behind us,
Lord of the years that stretch before,
Weaver of all the ties that bind us,
Keeper and King of the open door:
All through the seasons of sowing and reaping,
All through the harvest of song and tears,
Hold us close in Your tender keeping,
In Your arms let us dwell secure.

He who dwells in the shelter of the Most High will abide in the shadow of the Almighty. I will say to the Lord, "My refuge and my fortress, my God, in whom I trust."

PSALM 91:1–2 ESV

My Help

I will lift up mine eyes unto the hills,
from whence cometh my help.
My help cometh from the LORD,
which made heaven and earth.
He will not suffer thy foot to be moved:
he that keepeth thee will not slumber.
Behold, he that keepeth Israel
shall neither slumber nor sleep.
The LORD is thy keeper:
the LORD is thy shade upon thy right hand.
The sun shall not smite thee by day,
nor the moon by night.
The LORD shall preserve thee from all evil:
he shall preserve thy soul.
The LORD shall preserve thy going out
and thy coming in
from this time forth,
and even for evermore.

PSALM 121:1–8 KJV

We have a Father in heaven who is almighty, who loves His children as He loves His only-begotten Son, and whose very joy and delight it is to... help them at all times and under all circumstances.

GEORGE MUELLER

Shining Promises

Our feelings do not affect God's facts.
They may blow up, like clouds, and cover
the eternal things that we do most truly believe.
We may not see the shining of the promises—
but they still shine!
[His strength] is not for one moment less
because of our human weakness.

AMY CARMICHAEL

God's ways seem dark, but soon or late,
They touch the shining hills of day.

JOHN GREENLEAF WHITTIER

We do not know how this is true—
where would faith be if we did?—
but we do know that all things that happen
are full of shining seed.
Light is sown for us—not darkness.

But He knows the way I take; when He has tried me, I shall come forth as gold.

JOB 23:10 NASB

God Is Our Shield

Trust the LORD! He is your helper and your shield.

PSALM 115:9 NLT

Many are saying of my soul, there is no salvation
for him in God. But you, O LORD,
are a shield about me, my glory, and the lifter of my head.
I cried aloud to the LORD, and he answered me from his holy hill.

PSALM 3:2–4 ESV

Blessed be the LORD, my rock…he is my steadfast
love and my fortress, my stronghold and my deliverer,
my shield and he in whom I take refuge.

PSALM 144:1–2 ESV

Let the beloved of the LORD rest secure in him,
for he shields him all day long, and the one
the Lord loves rests between his shoulders.

DEUTERONOMY 33:12 NIV

*We are ever so secure in the
everlasting arms.*

God Knows

The simple fact of being…in the presence of the Lord
and of showing Him all that I think, feel, sense, and experience,
without trying to hide anything, must please Him.
Somehow, somewhere, I know that He loves me,
even though I do not feel that love
as I can feel a human embrace,
even though I do not hear a voice as I hear
human words of consolation….
God is greater than my senses, greater than my thoughts,
greater than my heart. I do believe that He
touches me in places that are unknown even to myself.

HENRI J. M. NOUWEN

Pour out your heart to God your Father.
He understands you better than you do.

God possesses infinite knowledge and an awareness
which is uniquely His. At all times,
even in the midst of any type of suffering,
I can realize that He knows,
loves, watches, understands,
and more than that, He has a purpose.

BILLY GRAHAM

But if anyone loves God, he is known by God.

1 CORINTHIANS 8:3 ESV

God's Care

The LORD is my shepherd; I shall not want.
He makes me to lie down in green pastures;
He leads me beside the still waters.
He restores my soul;
He leads me in the paths of righteousness
for His name's sake.
Yea, though I walk through
the valley of the shadow of death,
I will fear no evil;
For You are with me;
Your rod and Your staff, they comfort me.
You prepare a table before me
in the presence of my enemies:
You anoint my head with oil;
my cup runs over.
Surely goodness and mercy shall follow me
all the days of my life;
and I will dwell in the house of the LORD
Forever.

PSALM 23:1–6 NKJV

God never abandons anyone on whom He has set His love; nor does Christ, the good shepherd, ever lose track of His sheep.

J. I. PACKER

In the Silence

Our Father, sometimes Thou dost seem so far away,
as if Thou art a God in hiding,
as if Thou art determined
to elude all who seek Thee....
At times when we feel forsaken,
may we know the presence of the Holy Spirit
who brings comfort to all human hearts
when we are willing to surrender ourselves.

PETER MARSHALL

Be it ours, when we cannot see the face of God,
to trust under the shadow of His wings.

CHARLES H. SPURGEON

I believe in the sun even when it is not shining.
I believe in love even when I do not feel it.
I believe in God even when He is silent.

ON A WALL WHERE JEWS WERE
HIDDEN IN WWII

The eternal God is your refuge, and underneath are the everlasting arms.

DEUTERONOMY 33:27 NIV

God's Eternal Love

The LORD is like a father to his children,
tender and compassionate to those who fear him.
For he knows how weak we are;
he remembers we are only dust.
Our days on earth are like grass;
like wildflowers, we bloom and die.
The wind blows, and we are gone—
as though we had never been here.
But the love of the LORD remains forever....
The LORD has made the heavens his throne;
from there he rules over everything.

PSALM 103:13–17, 19 NLT

He remembered us in our weakness.
His faithful love endures forever.

PSALM 136:23 NLT

*Amid the ebb and flow of the passing world, our God remains unmoved,
and His throne endures forever.*

ROBERT COLEMAN

God Listens

Open wide the windows of our spirits
and fill us full of light;
open wide the door of our hearts,
that we may receive and entertain Thee
with all our powers of adoration.

CHRISTINA ROSSETTI

We come this morning—
Like empty pitchers to a full fountain,
With no merits of our own,
O Lord—open up a window of heaven…
And listen this morning.

JAMES WELDON JOHNSON

God listens in compassion and love,
just like we do when our
children come to us.
He delights in our presence.

RICHARD J. FOSTER

I love the Lord because he hears my voice and my prayer for mercy. Because he bends down to listen, I will pray as long as I have breath!

PSALM 116:1–2 NLT

Renewed Strength

Why do you say…"My way is hidden from the LORD;
my cause is disregarded by my God"?
Do you not know? Have you not heard?
The LORD is the everlasting God,
the Creator of the ends of the earth.
He will not grow tired or weary,
and his understanding no one can fathom.
Even youths grow tired and weary,
and young men stumble and fall;
but those who hope in the LORD
will renew their strength.
They will soar on wings like eagles;
they will run and not grow weary,
they will walk and not be faint.

ISAIAH 40:27–31 NIV

The LORD will give strength to His people;
the LORD will bless His people with peace.

PSALM 29:11 NKJV

What we need is not new light, but new sight;
not new paths, but new strength to walk in the old ones.

Always There

We need never shout across the spaces to an absent God.
He is nearer than our own soul,
closer than our most secret thoughts.

A. W. TOZER

God is always present in the temple of your heart...
His home.
And when you come in to meet Him there,
you find that it is the one place of deep satisfaction
where every longing is met.

Always be in a state of expectancy,
and see that you leave room
for God to come in as He likes.

OSWALD CHAMBERS

How ow lovely are Your dwelling places, O LORD of hosts! My soul longed
and even yearned for the courts of the LORD; my heart and my flesh sing for joy
to the living God.... For a day in Your courts is better than a thousand outside.

PSALM 84:1–2, 10 NASB

Rest in Him

My soul finds rest in God alone;
my salvation comes from him.
He alone is my rock and my salvation;
he is my fortress, I will never be shaken....
Find rest, O my soul, in God alone;
my hope comes from him.
He alone is my rock and my salvation;
he is my fortress, I will not be shaken.
My salvation and my honor depend on God;
he is my mighty rock, my refuge.
Trust in him at all times, O people;
pour out your hearts to him,
for God is our refuge....
One thing God has spoken,
two things have I heard:
that you, O God, are strong,
and that you, O Lord, are loving.

PSALM 62:1–2, 5–8, 11–12 NIV

Rest in the LORD, and wait patiently for him.

PSALM 37:7 KJV

When God finds a soul that rests in Him and is not easily moved...
to this same soul He gives the joy of His presence.

CATHERINE OF GENOA

Light in the Darkness

There is not enough darkness in all the world
to put out the light of one small candle....
In moments of discouragement, defeat,
or even despair,
there are always certain things to cling to.
Little things usually: remembered laughter,
the face of a sleeping child, a tree in the wind—
in fact, any reminder of
something deeply felt or dearly loved.
No one is so poor as not to have
many of these small candles.
When they are lighted, darkness goes away
and a touch of wonder remains.

ARTHUR GORDON

One taper lights a thousand,
Yet shines as it has shone;
And the humblest light may kindle
A brighter than its own.

HEZEKIAH BUTTERWORTH

It is you who light my lamp; the LORD my God lightens my darkness.

PSALM 18:28 ESV

God's Compassion

But this I call to mind,
and therefore I have hope:
The steadfast love of the LORD never ceases;
his mercies never come to an end;
they are new every morning;
great is your faithfulness.
"The LORD is my portion," says my soul,
"therefore I will hope in him."
The LORD is good to those who wait for him,
to the soul who seeks him....
For the Lord will not
cast off forever,
but, though he cause grief, he will have compassion
according to the abundance of his steadfast love;
for he does not willingly afflict
or grieve the children of men.

LAMENTATIONS 3:21–25, 31–33 ESV

LORD, don't hold back your tender mercies from me.
Let your unfailing love and faithfulness always protect me.

PSALM 40:11 NLT

The loving God we serve has immeasurable compassion and tenderness toward each of us throughout our lives.

JAMES DOBSON

Perfect Peace

Trials...may come in abundance. But they cannot penetrate into the sanctuary of the soul when it is settled in God, and we may dwell in perfect peace.

HANNAH WHITALL SMITH

What a friend we have in Jesus,
All our sins and griefs to bear;
What a privilege to carry
Everything to God in prayer.

O, what peace we often forfeit,
O, what needless pain we bear,
All because we do not carry
Everything to God in prayer.

GEORGE SCRIVEN

Night by night I will lie down and sleep in the thought of God.

WILLIAM MOUNTFORD

I will lie down and sleep in peace, for you alone, O Lord, make me dwell in safety.

PSALM 4:8 NIV

Seek the Lord

The God who made the world and everything in it is the
Lord of heaven and earth.... He himself gives all men
life and breath and everything else.... God did this so
that men would seek him and perhaps reach out for him
and find him, though he is not far from each one of us.
"For in him we live, and move, and have our being."

ACTS 17:24-25, 27-28 NIV

I love those who love me; and those who
diligently seek me will find me.

PROVERBS 8:17 NASB

Without faith it is impossible to please him,
for whoever would draw near to God must believe that
he exists and that he rewards those who seek him.

HEBREWS 11:6 ESV

*God is not an elusive dream or a phantom to chase, but a
divine person to know. He does not avoid us, but seeks us.
When we seek Him, the contact is instantaneous.*

NEVA COYLE

Totally Aware

God is every moment totally aware of each one of us.
Totally aware in intense concentration and love....
No one passes through any area of life, happy or tragic,
without the attention of God with him.

EUGENIA PRICE

Because God is responsible for our welfare, we are
told to cast all our care upon Him, for He cares for us.
God says, "I'll take the burden—don't give it a
thought—leave it to Me." God is keenly aware that
we are dependent upon Him for life's necessities.

BILLY GRAHAM

You are God's created beauty and the focus
of His affection and delight.

JANET L. WEAVER SMITH

Give all your worries and cares to God,
for he cares about you.

1 PETER 5:7 NLT

The Lord's Prayer

*F*ind a quiet, secluded place
so you won't be tempted to role-play before God.
Just be there as simply and honestly as you can manage.
The focus will shift from you to God,
and you will begin to sense his grace....
This is your Father you are dealing with,
and he knows better than you what you need.
With a God like this loving you,
you can pray very simply.

MATTHEW 6:6, 8–9 THE MESSAGE

*O*ur Father which art in heaven,
Hallowed be thy name.
Thy kingdom come.
Thy will be done in earth, as it is in heaven.
Give us this day our daily bread.
And forgive us our debts, as we forgive our debtors.
And lead us not into temptation, but deliver us from evil:
For thine is the kingdom, and the power,
and the glory, for ever. Amen.

MATTHEW 6:9–13 KJV

They who seek the throne of grace find that throne in every place;
If we live a life of prayer, God is present everywhere.

OLIVER HOLDEN

Steps of Faith

In the dark dreary nights,
when the storm is at its most fierce,
the lighthouse burns bright
so the sailors can find their way home again.
In life the same light burns.
This light is fueled with love, faith, and hope.
And through life's most fierce storms
these three burn their brightest
so we also can find our way home again.

Why should we live halfway up the hill and swathed in the mists,
when we might have an unclouded sky and a radiant sun over our
heads if we would climb higher and walk in the light of His face?

ALEXANDER MACLAREN

Faith goes up the stairs that love has made and looks
out the window which hope has opened.

CHARLES H. SPURGEON

*Let us draw near to God.... Let us hold unswervingly to the
hope we profess, for he who promised is faithful.*

HEBREWS 10:22–23 NIV

The Grace of God

But God, being rich in mercy,
because of His great love with which He loved us,
even when we were dead in our transgressions,
made us alive together with Christ
(by grace you have been saved),
and raised us up with Him, and seated us with Him
in the heavenly places in Christ Jesus,
so that in the ages to come He might show
the surpassing riches of His grace
in kindness toward us in Christ Jesus.
For by grace you have been saved through faith;
and that not of yourselves, it is the gift of God;
not as a result of works, so that no one may boast.
For we are His workmanship,
created in Christ Jesus for good works,
which God prepared beforehand
so that we would walk in them.

EPHESIANS 2:4–10 NASB

From his fullness we have all received,
grace upon grace.

JOHN 1:16 ESV

*Grace means that God already loves us as much
as an infinite God can possibly love.*

PHILIP YANCEY

His Presence

And I have felt
A presence that disturbs me with the joy
Of elevated thoughts; a sense sublime
Of something far more deeply interfused,
Whose dwelling is the light of setting suns.

WILLIAM WORDSWORTH

Know by the light of faith
that God is present,
and be content with directing
all your actions toward Him.

BROTHER LAWRENCE

God wants us to be present where we are.
He invites us to see and to hear what is
around us and, through it all,
to discern the footprints of the Holy.

RICHARD J. FOSTER

The Lord your God is with you, he is mighty to save.... He will take great delight in you, he will quiet you with his love, he will rejoice over you with singing.

ZEPHANIAH 3:17 NIV

The Stronghold

The LORD is my light and my salvation—
whom shall I fear?
The LORD is the stronghold of my life—
of whom shall I be afraid?…
One thing I ask of the LORD, this is what I seek:
that I may dwell in the house of the LORD
all the days of my life,
to gaze upon the beauty of the LORD
and to seek him in his temple.
For in the day of trouble
he will keep me safe in his dwelling;
he will hide me in the shelter of his tabernacle
and set me high upon a rock.…
Hear my voice when I call, O LORD;
be merciful to me and answer me.
My heart says of you, "Seek his face!"
Your face, LORD, I will seek.

PSALM 27:1, 4–5, 7–8 NIV

Do not hide your face from your servant;
answer me quickly, for I am in trouble.
Come near and rescue me.

PSALM 69:17–18 NIV

*Leave behind your fear and dwell on the lovingkindness of God,
that you may recover by gazing on Him.*

Comfort Sweet

There is a place of comfort sweet
Near to the heart of God,
A place where we our Savior meet,
Near to the heart of God....
Hold us who wait before Thee
Near to the heart of God.

CLELAND B. MCAFEE

You will never find Jesus so precious as when
the world is one vast, howling wilderness.
Then He is like a rose blooming
in the midst of the desolation,
a rock rising above the storm.

ROBERT MURRAY M'CHEYNE

God comforts. He lays His right hand
on the wounded soul...
and He says, as if that one
were the only soul in all the universe:
O greatly beloved, fear not:
peace be unto thee.

AMY CARMICHAEL

The LORD is my light and my salvation; whom shall I fear?

PSALM 27:1 KJV

I Will Help You

"So do not fear, for I am with you;
do not be dismayed, for I am your God.
I will strengthen you and help you;
I will uphold you with my righteous right hand....
"For I am the LORD, your God,
who takes hold of your right hand and says to you,
Do not fear; I will help you.
Do not be afraid...for I myself will help you,"
declares the LORD, your Redeemer,
the Holy One of Israel.

ISAIAH 41:10, 13–14 NIV

For he hath said, I will never leave thee,
nor forsake thee. So that we may boldly say,
The Lord is my helper, and I will not fear.

HEBREWS 13:5–6 KJV

God's strength will always be your
strength in your hour of need.

The Sea Remains the Sea

Dear Lord, today I thought of the words
of Vincent van Gogh,
"It is true that there is an ebb and flow,
but the sea remains the sea."
You are the sea. Although I may experience
many ups and downs in my emotions
and often feel great shifts in my inner life,
You remain the same....
There are days of sadness and days of joy;
there are feelings of guilt and feelings of gratitude;
there are moments of failure and moments of success;
but all of them are embraced by Your unwavering love.
My only real temptation is to doubt Your love...
to remove myself from the healing radiance of Your love.
To do these things is to move into the darkness of despair.
O Lord, sea of love and goodness,
let me not fear too much
the storms and winds of my daily life,
and let me know that there is ebb and flow...
but that the sea remains the sea.
Amen.

HENRI J. M. NOUWEN

You rule over the surging sea; when its waves mount up, you still them.

Faithfulness Extended

*Y*our steadfast love, O LORD,
    extends to the heavens,
your faithfulness to the clouds.

PSALM 36:5 ESV

*R*emember your promise to me;
    it is my only hope.
Your promise revives me;
    it comforts me in all my troubles....
I meditate on your age-old regulations;
    O LORD, they comfort me....
Your decrees have been the theme
    of my song wherever I have lived.
I reflect at night on who you are, O LORD;
    therefore, I obey your instructions....
Your eternal word, O LORD, stands firm in heaven.
Your faithfulness extends to every generation,
    as enduring as the earth you created.

PSALM 119:49-50, 52, 54-55, 89-90 NLT

Swim through your troubles. Run to the promises, they are our Lord's branches hanging over the water so that His children may take a grip of them.

SAMUEL RUTHERFORD

Trust God's Heart

He writes in characters too grand
for our short sight to understand.
We catch but broken strokes
and try to fathom all the withered hopes
Of death, of life,
the endless war, the useless strife....
But there, with larger, clearer sight, we shall see this:
His way was right.

JOHN OXENHAM

In those times I can't seem to find God, I rest in the
assurance He knows how to find me.

NEVA COYLE

Wait upon God's strengthening, and say to Him,
"O Lord, You have been our refuge in all generations."
Trust in Him who has placed this burden on you.
What you yourself cannot bear,
bear with the help of God who is all-powerful.

BONIFACE

Lord, You have been our dwelling place in all generations....
Even from everlasting to everlasting, You are God.

PSALM 90:1–2 NASB

Don't Be Afraid

Don't be afraid, I've redeemed you.
I've called your name. You're mine.
When you're in over your head, I'll be there with you.
When you're in rough waters, you will not go down.
When you're between a rock and a hard place,
it won't be a dead end—
because I am God, your personal God,
The Holy of Israel, your Savior.
I paid a huge price for you…!
That's how much you mean to me!
That's how much I love you!

ISAIAH 43:1–4 THE MESSAGE

Do not be afraid. I am the First and the Last.
I am the Living One; I was dead,
and behold I am alive for ever and ever!

REVELATION 1:17–18 NIV

If God be for us, who can be against us?

ROMANS 8:31 KJV

Do not be afraid to enter the cloud that is settling down on your life. God is in it. The other side is radiant with His glory.

L. B. COWMAN

God's Answers

I asked for strength that I might achieve;
I was made weak that I might learn humbly to obey.
I asked for health that I might do greater things;
I was given infirmity that I might do better things.
I asked for riches that I might be wise.
I asked for power that I might feel the need of God.
I asked for all things that I might enjoy all things.
I got nothing that I asked for,
But everything that I had hoped for.
Almost despite myself my unspoken prayers were answered;
I am, among all people, most richly blessed.

UNKNOWN CONFEDERATE SOLDIER

We shall come one day to a heaven where we
shall gratefully know that God's great refusals were
sometimes the true answers to our truest prayer.

P. T. FORSYTH

For now we see in a mirror dimly, but then face to face; now I know in part, but then I will know fully just as I also have been fully known.

1 CORINTHIANS 13:12 NASB

Intercession

If you don't know what you're doing,
pray to the Father. He loves to help.

JAMES 1:5 THE MESSAGE

And the Holy Spirit helps us in our weakness.
For example, we don't know what God wants us
to pray for. But the Holy Spirit prays for us with
groanings that cannot be expressed in words.
And the Father who knows all hearts knows what
the Spirit is saying, for the Spirit pleads for us
believers in harmony with God's own will.
And we know that God causes everything to
work together for the good of those who love God
and are called according to his purpose for them.

ROMANS 8:26–28 NLT

When life tumbles in and problems overwhelm us...how reassuring it is to know that the Spirit makes intercession for us!

HAZEL C. LEE

Overcoming

Christ desires to be with you in
whatever crisis you may find yourself.
Call upon His name. See if He will not
do as He promised He would.
He will not make your problems go away,
but He will give you the power to
deal with and overcome them….
Suffering is endurable if we do not
have to bear it alone;
and the more compassionate the Presence,
the less acute the pain.

BILLY GRAHAM

He did not say, "You will never have a rough passage,
you will never be over-strained,
you will never feel uncomfortable,"
but He did say, "You will never be overcome."

JULIAN OF NORWICH

The world is full of suffering.
It is also full of the overcoming of it.

HELEN KELLER

I have told you these things, so that in me you may have peace. In this world you will have trouble. But take heart! I have overcome the world.

JOHN 16:33 NIV

Fresh Hope

God…rekindles burned-out lives with fresh hope,
restoring dignity and respect to their lives—
a place in the sun!
For the very structures of earth are God's;
he has laid out his operations on a firm foundation.

1 Samuel 2:7–8 the message

We put our hope in the Lord.
He is our help and our shield. In him our
hearts rejoice, for we trust in his holy name.
Let your unfailing love surround us, Lord,
for our hope is in you alone.

Psalm 33:18–22 nlt

Trust steadily in God, hope unswervingly,
love extravagantly.

1 Corinthians 13:13 the message

Though seen through many a tear,
Let not my star of hope grow dim or disappear.

BENJAMIN SCHMOLCK

Every Need

God wants nothing from us except our needs,
and these furnish Him with room
to display His bounty when He supplies them freely....
Not what I have, but what I do not have,
is the first point of contact between my soul and God.

CHARLES H. SPURGEON

Jesus Christ has brought every need, every joy,
every gratitude, every hope of ours before God.
He accompanies us and brings us
into the presence of God.

DIETRICH BONHOEFFER

The "air" which our souls need also envelops
all of us at all times and on all sides.
God is round about us...on every hand,
with many-sided and all-sufficient grace.

OLE HALLESBY

My God is changeless in his love for me and he will come and help me.

PSALM 59:10 TLB

Restoration

On the day I called, You answered me;
You made me bold
with strength in my soul....
For great is the glory of the LORD....
Though I walk in the midst of trouble,
You will revive me;
You will stretch forth Your hand...
and Your right hand will save me.
The LORD will accomplish what concerns me;
Your lovingkindness,
O LORD, is everlasting;
do not forsake the works of Your hands.

PSALM 138:3, 5, 7-8 NASB

Weeping may remain for a night,
but rejoicing comes in the morning.

PSALM 30:5 NIV

I have suffered much, O LORD;
restore my life again as you promised.

PSALM 119:107 NLT

How calmly may we commit ourselves to the hands
of Him who bears up the world.

JEAN PAUL RICHTER

Settled in Solitude

Solitude liberates us from entanglements by
carving out a space from which we can see
ourselves and our situation before the Audience of One.
Solitude provides the private place where
we can take our bearings and so
make God our North Star.

OS GUINNESS

Settle yourself in solitude and you will
come upon Him in yourself.

TERESA OF AVILA

We must drink deeply from the very Source the deep calm
and peace of interior quietude and refreshment of God,
allowing the pure water of divine grace to flow
plentifully and unceasingly from the Source itself.

MOTHER TERESA

Whoever drinks of the water that I will give him shall never thirst; but the water that I will give him will become in him a well of water springing up to eternal life.

JOHN 4:14 NASB

The Goodness of God

I would have despaired unless I had believed
that I would see the goodness of the LORD
in the land of the living.
Wait for the LORD;
be strong and let your heart take courage;
yes, wait for the LORD.

PSALM 27:13–14 NASB

Be strong and courageous! Do not be afraid....
For the LORD your God will personally go ahead of you.
He will neither fail you nor abandon you.

DEUTERONOMY 31:6 NLT

He loveth righteousness and judgment:
the earth is full of the goodness of the LORD.

PSALM 33:5 KJV

God is not merely good, but goodness;
goodness is not merely divine, but God.

C. S. LEWIS

His Beautiful World

The God who holds the whole world in His hands
wraps Himself in the splendor of the sun's light
and walks among the clouds.

Forbid that I should walk through
Thy beautiful world with unseeing eyes:
Forbid that the lure of the market-place
should ever entirely steal my heart away from
the love of the open acres and the green trees:
Forbid that under the low roof of workshop
or office or study I should ever forget
Thy great overarching sky.

JOHN BAILLIE

Our Creator would never have made such lovely days,
and given us the deep hearts to enjoy them,
above and beyond all thought,
unless we were meant to be immortal.

NATHANIEL HAWTHORNE

The whole earth is full of his glory.

ISAIAH 6:3 KJV

God's Peace

Let not your heart be troubled:
ye believe in God, believe also in me.
In my Father's house are many mansions:
if it were not so, I would have told you.
I go to prepare a place for you.
And if I go and prepare a place for you,
I will come again, and receive you unto myself;
that where I am, there ye may be also....
I will not leave you comfortless: I will come to you....
Peace I leave with you, my peace I give unto you:
not as the world giveth, give I unto you.
Let not your heart be troubled, neither let it be afraid.

JOHN 14:1–3, 18, 27 KJV

And the God of love and peace shall be with you.

2 CORINTHIANS 13:11 KJV

*May the God of love and peace set your heart at rest
and speed you on your journey.*

RAYMOND OF PENYAFORT

Source of Wonder

I would maintain that thanks are
the highest form of thought, and that
gratitude is happiness doubled by wonder.

G. K. CHESTERTON

*D*ear Lord, grant me the grace of wonder.
Surprise me, amaze me,
awe me in every crevice of Your universe....
Each day enrapture me
with Your marvelous things without number.
I do not ask to see the reason for it all;
I ask only to share the wonder of it all.

JOSHUA ABRAHAM HESCHEL

*M*ay our lives be illumined
by the steady radiance
renewed daily,
of a wonder,
the source of which
is beyond reason.

DAG HAMMARSKJÖLD

I will give thanks to the Lord with all my heart; I will tell of all Your wonders.
I will be glad and exult in You; I will sing praise to Your name, O Most High.

PSALM 9:1–2 NASB

Shepherd and Guardian

I am the good shepherd.
I know my own and my own know me,
just as the Father knows me and I know the Father;
and I lay down my life for the sheep.

JOHN 10:14–15 ESV

He shall feed his flock like a shepherd:
he shall gather the lambs with his arm,
and carry them in his bosom,
and shall gently lead those that are with young.

ISAIAH 40:11 KJV

All we like sheep have gone astray;
we have turned every one to his own way;
and the LORD hath laid on him the iniquity of us all.

ISAIAH 53:6 KJV

You were continually straying like sheep,
but now you have returned to the
Shepherd and Guardian of your souls.

1 PETER 2:25 NASB

*Genuine love sees faces, not a mass: the Good Shepherd
calls His own sheep by name.*

GEORGE A. BUTTRICK

Nothing but Grace

There is nothing but God's grace.
We walk upon it; we breathe it;
we live and die by it;
it makes the nails and axles of the universe.

ROBERT LOUIS STEVENSON

Grace is no stationary thing, it is ever becoming.
It is flowing straight out of God's heart.
Grace does nothing but re-form and convey God.
Grace makes the soul conformable to the will of God.
God, the ground of the soul, and grace go together.

MEISTER ECKHART

Grace and gratitude belong together like heaven and earth.
Grace evokes gratitude like the voice an echo.
Gratitude follows grace as thunder follows lightning.

KARL BARTH

GOD is sheer mercy and grace; not easily angered, he's rich in love....
As far as sunrise is from sunset, he has separated us from our sins.

PSALM 103:8, 12 THE MESSAGE

Hope in God

Why are you in despair, O my soul?
And why have you become disturbed within me?
Hope in God, for I shall again praise Him
for the help of His presence.
O my God, my soul is in despair within me;
therefore I remember You....
Deep calls to deep at the sound of Your waterfalls;
all Your breakers and Your waves have rolled over me.
The LORD will command His lovingkindness in the daytime;
and His song will be with me in the night,
a prayer to the God of my life.

PSALM 42:5–8 NASB

He won't brush aside the bruised and the hurt
and he won't disregard the small and insignificant,
but he'll steadily and firmly set things right.

ISAIAH 42:3 THE MESSAGE

Hope is faith holding out its hands in the dark.

GEORGE ILES

Faithful Guide

God, who has led you safely on so far,
will lead you on to the end.
Be altogether at rest in the loving holy confidence
which you ought to have in His heavenly Providence.

FRANCIS DE SALES

Guidance is a sovereign act. Not merely does God will
to guide us   by showing us His way…
whatever mistakes we may make, we shall come safely home.
Slippings and strayings there will be, no doubt,
but the everlasting arms are beneath us;
we shall be caught, rescued, restored.
This is God's promise; this is how good He is.
And our self-distrust, while keeping us humble,
must not cloud the joy with which
we lean on our faithful covenant God.

J. I. PACKER

*When we obey him, every path he guides us on is fragrant
with his loving-kindness and his truth.*

PSALM 25:10 TLB

God Is Our Refuge

Hear my cry, O God; Give heed to my prayer.
From the end of the earth I call to You
when my heart is faint;
lead me to the rock that is higher than I.
For You have been a refuge for me,
a tower of strength against the enemy.
Let me dwell in Your tent forever;
let me take refuge in the shelter of Your wings.

PSALM 61:1–4 NASB

Whom have I in heaven but You?
And besides You, I desire nothing on earth.
My flesh and my heart may fail,
but God is the strength of my heart and my portion forever....
As for me, the nearness of God is my good;
I have made the Lord GOD my refuge.

PSALM 73:25–26, 28 NASB

When God has become…our refuge and our fortress, then we can reach out to Him in the midst of a broken world and feel at home while still on the way.

HENRI J. M. NOUWEN

Seeing by Faith

Living a life of faith means
never knowing where you are being led.
But it does mean loving and knowing
the One who is leading.
It is literally a life of faith,
not of understanding and reason—
a life of knowing Him who calls us to go.

OSWALD CHAMBERS

Where reasons are given, we don't need faith.
Where only darkness surrounds us,
we have no means for seeing except by faith.

ELISABETH ELLIOT

Trust God where you cannot trace Him.
Do not try to penetrate the cloud He brings over you;
rather look to the bow that is on it.
The mystery is God's; the promise is yours.

JOHN MACDUFF

The secret things belong unto the LORD our God:
but those things which are revealed
belong unto us and to our children for ever.

DEUTERONOMY 29:29 KJV

God's Power

I pray that out of his glorious riches
he may strengthen you with power
through his Spirit in your inner being,
so that Christ may dwell in your hearts through faith.
And I pray that you, being rooted and established in love,
may have power, together with all the saints,
to grasp how wide and long and
high and deep is the love of Christ,
and to know this love that surpasses knowledge—
that you may be filled to the measure
of all the fullness of God.
Now to him who is able to do
immeasurably more than all we ask or imagine,
according to his power that is at work within us,
to him be glory in the church and in
Christ Jesus throughout all generations,
for ever and ever! Amen.

EPHESIANS 3:16–21 NIV

In his great mercy he has given us new birth
into a living hope…kept in heaven for you,
who through faith are shielded by God's power.

1 PETER 1:3–5 NIV

God is with us, and His power is around us.

CHARLES H. SPURGEON

He Carries Our Sorrows

Your tears are precious to God.
They are like stained-glass
windows in the darkness,
whose true beauty is revealed
only when there is a light within.

There is a sacredness in tears.
They are not the mark of weakness, but of power.
They speak more eloquently than ten thousand tongues.
They are the messengers of overwhelming grief,
of deep contrition, and of unspeakable love.

WASHINGTON IRVING

When Jesus…confides to us that
He is "acquainted with
Grief," we listen, for that also is an
Acquaintance of our own.

EMILY DICKINSON

A teardrop on earth summons the King of Heaven.

CHARLES R. SWINDOLL

Surely he hath borne our griefs, and carried our sorrows...
and with his stripes we are healed.

ISAIAH 53:4–5 KJV

The Presence of God

I look behind me and you're there,
then up ahead andyou're there, too—
your reassuring presence, coming and going.
This is too much, too wonderful—
I can't take it all in!

PSALM 139:5–6 THE MESSAGE

Where can I go from your Spirit?
Where can I flee from your presence?
If I go up to the heavens, you are there;
if I make my bed in the depths, you are there.
If I rise on the wings of the dawn,
if I settle on the far side of the sea,
even there your hand will guide me,
your right hand will hold me fast.

PSALM 139:7–10 NIV

I am with you and will watch over you
wherever you go.

GENESIS 28:15 NIV

Each one of us is encircled by the presence of Almighty God.

CHARLES STANLEY

Enfolded in Peace

I will let God's peace infuse every part of today.
As the chaos swirls and life's demands pull at me
on all sides, I will breathe in God's peace
that surpasses all understanding.
He has promised that He would
set within me a peace too deeply planted
to be affected by unexpected or exhausting demands.

WENDY MOORE

Calm me, O Lord, as you stilled the storm,
Still me, O Lord, keep me from harm.
Let all the tumult within me cease,
Enfold me, Lord, in your peace.

CELTIC TRADITIONAL

God cannot give us a happiness and peace apart from Himself,
because it is not there. There is no such thing.

C. S. LEWIS

God's peace…is far more wonderful than the human mind can understand.
His peace will keep your thoughts and your hearts quiet and at rest.

PHILIPPIANS 4:7 TLB

God's Sovereignty

Even though the fig trees have no blossoms,
and there are no grapes on the vines;
even though the olive crop fails,
and the fields lie empty and barren;
even though the flocks die in the fields,
and the cattle barns are empty,
yet I will rejoice in the LORD!
I will be joyful in the God of my salvation!
The Sovereign LORD is my strength!

HABAKKUK 3:17–19 NLT

Wealth and honor come from you;
you are the ruler of all things.
In your hands are strength and power
to exalt and give strength to all.
Now, our God, we give you thanks,
and praise your glorious name.

1 CHRONICLES 29:12–13 NIV

Trials have no value or intrinsic meaning in themselves. It's the way we respond to those trials that makes all the difference.

JONI EARECKSON TADA

God Draws Near

When you are lonely
I wish you love;
When you are down
I wish you joy;
When you are troubled
I wish you peace;
When things are complicated
I wish you simple beauty;
When things are chaotic
I wish you inner silence;
When things seem empty
I wish you hope,
And the sweet sense of God's presence
every passing day.

God still draws near to us in the ordinary,
commonplace, everyday experiences
and places…. He comes in surprising ways.

HENRY GARIEPY

I have set the LORD always before me:
because he is at my right hand, I shall not be moved.

PSALM 16:8 KJV

Have Mercy

Search me, O God, and know my heart;
test me and know my anxious thoughts.
See if there is any offensive way in me,
and lead me in the way everlasting.

PSALM 139:23–24 NIV

When my anxious thoughts multiply within me,
Your consolations delight my soul.

PSALM 94:19 NASB

Seek the LORD while you can find him.
Call on him now while he is near.
Let the wicked change their ways
and banish the very thought of doing wrong.
Let them turn to the LORD that he may have mercy on them.
Yes, turn to our God, for he will forgive generously.

ISAIAH 55:6–7 NLT

We need more than a watchmaker who winds up the universe
and lets it tick. We need love and mercy and forgiveness
and grace—qualities only a personal God can offer.

PHILIP YANCEY

Grace for Trials

God has not promised skies always blue,
flower-strewn pathways all our lives through;
God has not promised sun without rain,
joy without sorrow, peace without pain.
But God has promised strength for the day,
rest for the labor, light for the way,
grace for the trials, help from above,
unfailing sympathy, undying love.

ANNIE JOHNSON FLINT

After winter comes the summer.
After night comes the dawn.
And after every storm,
there comes clear, open skies.

SAMUEL RUTHERFORD

They that sow in tears shall reap in joy.

PSALM 126:5 KJV

The Love of God

The LORD is merciful and compassionate,
slow to get angry and filled with unfailing love.
The LORD is good to everyone.
He showers compassion on all his creation.

PSALM 145:8–9 NLT

Who shall separate us from the love of Christ?
Shall trouble or hardship or persecution
or famine or nakedness or danger or sword?…
No, in all these things we are more than conquerors
through him who loved us.
For I am convinced that neither death nor life,
neither angels nor demons,
neither the present nor the future, nor any powers,
neither height nor depth, nor anything else in all creation,
will be able to separate us from the love of God
that is in Christ Jesus our Lord.

ROMANS 8:35, 37-39 NIV

Nothing can separate you from His love, absolutely nothing....
God is enough for time, and God is enough for eternity. God is enough!

HANNAH WHITALL SMITH

Waiting Quietly

Dear Father, I have so many questions and so few answers.
Reveal to me Your will. Show me Your path
and give me the wisdom to follow it.
Feed me from Your word, O Lord,
and teach me Your ways.
When the questions of life are confusing or
overwhelming, remind me to wait on You,
the One who has all the answers. Amen.

MARILYN JANSEN

In waiting we begin to get in touch with the rhythms of life—
stillness and action, listening and decision. They are the
rhythms of God. It is in the everyday and the commonplace
that we learn patience, acceptance, and contentment.

RICHARD J. FOSTER

When you get into a tight place and everything goes against you,
till it seems as though you could not hang on a minute longer,
never give up then, for that is just the place and time
that the tide will turn.

HARRIET BEECHER STOWE

I wait for the LORD, my soul waits, and in his word I put my hope. My soul waits for the Lord more than watchmen wait for the morning.

PSALM 130:5–6 NIV

Renewing Word

*Y*ou're my place of quiet retreat;
I wait for your Word to renew me....
Therefore I lovingly embrace everything you say.

PSALM 119:114, 119 THE MESSAGE

*Y*ou have dealt well with Your servant, O LORD,
according to Your word.
Teach me good discernment and knowledge,
for I believe in Your commandments.
Before I was afflicted I went astray,
but now I keep Your word.
You are good and do good; teach me Your statutes.

PSALM 119:65–68 NASB

*A*ll your words are true;
all your righteous laws are eternal.

PSALM 119:160 NIV

*T*he LORD is faithful in all his words
and kind in all his works.

PSALM 145:13 ESV

Be still, and in the quiet moments, listen to the voice of your heavenly Father. His words can renew your spirit…no one knows you and your needs like He does.

JANET L. WEAVER SMITH

His Imprint

The God of the universe—
the One who created everything and
holds it all in His hand—
created each of us in His image,
to bear His likeness, His imprint.
It is only when Christ dwells within our hearts,
radiating the pure light of His love through our humanity,
that we discover who we are and
what we were intended to be.

WENDY MOORE

In the very beginning it was God who formed us
by His Word. He made us in His own image.
God was spirit and He gave us a spirit
so that He could come into us and mingle
His own life with our life.

MADAME JEANNE GUYON

Made in His image, we can have real meaning,
and we can have real knowledge through
what He has communicated to us.

FRANCIS SCHAEFFER

For in Him all the fullness of Deity dwells in bodily form,
and in Him you have been made complete.

COLOSSIANS 2:9 NASB

Strength in Suffering

And the Lord God will wipe away tears
from off all faces.

ISAIAH 25:8 KJV

We also rejoice in our sufferings,
because we know that suffering produces perseverance;
perseverance, character; and character, hope.
And hope does not disappoint us, because
God has poured out his
love into our hearts by the Holy Spirit,
whom he has given us.

ROMANS 5:3–5 NIV

That I may know him,
and the power of his resurrection,
and the fellowship of his sufferings.

PHILIPPIANS 3:10 KJV

Character cannot be developed in ease and quiet. Only through experience of trial and suffering can the soul be strengthened.

HELEN KELLER

For Himself

Although it be good to think upon the kindness of God,
and to love Him and worship Him for it;
yet it is far better to gaze upon the pure essence of Him
and to love Him and worship Him for Himself.

We desire many things,
and [God] offers us only one thing.
He can offer us only one thing—Himself.
He has nothing else to give.
There is nothing else to give.

PETER KREEFT

The reason for loving God is God Himself,
and the measure in which we should love Him
is to love Him without measure.

BERNARD OF CLAIRVAUX

The Lord alone shall be exalted.

ISAIAH 2:11 KJV

The Word of God

For as the rain and the snow come down from heaven
and do not return there but water the earth,
making it bring forth and sprout,
giving seed to the sower and bread to the eater,
so shall my word be that goes out from my mouth;
it shall not return to me empty,
but it shall accomplish that which I purpose,
and shall succeed in the thing for which I sent it.

ISAIAH 55:10–11 ESV

Not one word has failed of all His good promise.

1 KINGS 8:56 NASB

The fulfillment of God's promise
depends entirely on trusting God and his way,
and then simply embracing him and what he does.
God's promise arrives as pure gift.

ROMANS 4:16 THE MESSAGE

God is the God of promise. He keeps His word,
even when that seems impossible.

COLIN URQUHART

Take Refuge

Let my soul take refuge…
beneath the shadow of Your wings:
let my heart, this sea of restless waves,
find peace in You, O God.

AUGUSTINE

My Good Shepherd, who have shown
Your very gentle mercy to us…
give grace and strength to me,
Your little lamb, that in no tribulation
or anguish or pain may I turn away from You.

FRANCIS OF ASSISI

God stands fast as your rock, steadfast as your safeguard,
sleepless as your watcher, valiant as your champion.

CHARLES H. SPURGEON

Why would God promise a refuge unless He knew we
would need a place to hide once in a while?

NEVA COYLE

The LORD is good, a refuge in times of trouble.
He cares for those who trust in him.

NAHUM 1:7 NIV

Incomparable Blessings

I keep asking that the God of our Lord Jesus Christ,
the glorious Father, may give you
the Spirit of wisdom and revelation,
so that you may know him better.
I pray also that the eyes of your heart
may be enlightened in order that
you may know the hope to which he has called you,
the riches of his glorious inheritance in the saints,
and his incomparably great power for us who believe.

EPHESIANS 1:17–19 NIV

The LORD is great, and greatly to be praised....
The LORD made the heavens.
Honour and majesty are before him:
strength and beauty are in his sanctuary....
Give unto the LORD glory and strength.
Give unto the LORD the glory due unto his name.

PSALM 96:4–8 KJV

Strength, rest, guidance, grace, help, sympathy, love—all from God to us!
What a list of blessings!

EVELYN STENBOCK

Sweet Hour of Prayer

Sweet hour of prayer, sweet hour of prayer,
That calls me from a world of care,
And bids me at my Father's throne,
Make all my wants and wishes known!
In seasons of distress and grief,
My soul has often found relief,
And oft escaped the tempter's snare
By thy return, sweet hour of prayer.

WILLIAM W. WALFORD

God understands our prayers even when we
can't find the words to say them.

If we knew how to listen, we would hear Him
speaking to us. For God does speak....
If we knew how to listen to God,
if we knew how to look around us,
our whole life would become prayer.

MICHAEL QUOIST

I call on you, O God, for you will answer me;
give ear to me and hear my prayer.

PSALM 17:6 NIV

Everlasting Light

The sun will no more
be your light by day,
nor will the brightness of the moon shine on you,
for the LORD will be your everlasting light,
and your God will be your glory.
Your sun will never set again,
and your moon will wane no more;
the LORD will beyour everlasting light,
and your days of sorrow will end.

ISAIAH 60:19–20 NIV

Light arises in the darkness for the upright; He is
gracious and compassionate and righteous.

PSALM 112:4 NASB

Those who have met God are not looking for something—they have found it; they are not searching for light—upon them the Light has already shined.

A. W. TOZER

Love One Another

You who have received so much love
share it with others.
Love others the way that God has loved you,
with tenderness.

MOTHER TERESA

Let Jesus be in your heart,
Eternity in your spirit,
The world under your feet,
The will of God in your actions.
And let the love of God shine forth from you.

CATHERINE OF GENOA

Every single act of love
bears the imprint of God.

Dear friends, since God so loved us, we also ought to love one another....
If we love one another, God lives in us and his love is made complete in us.

1 JOHN 4:11–12 NIV

No More Tears

Those who sow in tears
shall reap with shouts of joy!
He who goes out weeping,
bearing the seed for sowing,
shall come home with shouts of joy,
bringing his sheaves with him.

PSALM 126:5-6 ESV

And I heard a loud voice from the throne saying,
"Now the dwelling of God is with men,
and he will live with them.
They will be his people, and God himself
will be with them and be their God.
He will wipe every tear from their eyes.
There will be no more death or mourning
or crying or pain,
for the old order of things has passed away."
He who was seated on the throne said,
"I am making everything new....
I am the Alpha and the Omega,
the Beginning and the End."

REVELATION 21:3–6 NIV

The implications of the name Immanuel are comforting....
He desires to weep with us and to wipe away our tears.

MICHAEL CARD

The Beauty of God's Peace

In comparison with this big world,
the human heart is only a small thing.
Though the world is so large,
it is utterly unable to satisfy this tiny heart.
Our ever growing soul and its capacities
can be satisfied only in the infinite God.
As water is restless until it reaches its level,
so the soul has no peace until it rests in God.

SADHU SUNDAR SINGH

Peace is a margin of power around our daily need.
Peace is a consciousness of springs too deep
for earthly droughts to dry up.

HARRY EMERSON FOSDICK

Drop Thy still dews of quietness
till all our strivings cease;
take from our souls the strain and stress,
and let our ordered lives confess
the beauty of Thy peace.

JOHN GREENLEAF WHITTIER

Be still, and know that I am God.

PSALM 46:10 KJV

The Power of God

Search high and low, scan skies and land,
you'll find nothing and no one quite like GOD.
The holy angels are in awe before him;
he looms immense and august
over everyone around him.
GOD of the Angel Armies, who is like you,
powerful and faithful from every angle?

PSALM 89:6–8 THE MESSAGE

Yours, O LORD, is the greatness and the power and the glory
and the majesty and the splendor, for everything
in heaven and earth is yours. Yours, O LORD,
is the kingdom; you are exalted as head over all.

1 CHRONICLES 29:11 NIV

Ah, Sovereign LORD, you have made the heavens
and the earth by your great power and outstretched arm.
Nothing is too hard for you.

JEREMIAH 32:17 NIV

Whatever the circumstances, whatever the call…His strength will be your strength in your hour of need.

BILLY GRAHAM

That I May Know Him

Lord Jesus Christ...
May I know You more clearly,
Love You more dearly
And follow You more nearly
Day by day. Amen.

RICHARD OF CHICHESTER

Give us, Lord: a pure heart that we may see Thee,
a humble heart that we may hear Thee,
a heart of love that we may serve Thee,
a heart of faith that we may live with Thee.

DAG HAMMARSKJÖLD

God be in my head, and in my understanding;
God be in my eyes, and in my looking;
God be in my mouth, and in my speaking;
God be in my heart, and in my thinking;
God be at my end, and at my departing.

If you are pleased with me, teach me your ways so I may know you and continue to find favor with you.

EXODUS 33:13 NIV

Our Gracious God

Yet the LORD longs to be gracious to you;
he rises to show you compassion.
For the LORD is a God of justice.
Blessed are all who wait for him!

ISAIAH 30:18 NIV

He made known his ways to Moses,
his deeds to the people of Israel:
The LORD is compassionate and gracious,
slow to anger, abounding in love.

PSALM 103:7–8 NIV

O LORD, be gracious to us; we long for you.
Be our strength every morning,
our salvation in time of distress.

ISAIAH 33:2 NIV

Lord...give me only Your love and Your grace. With this I am rich enough, and I have no more to ask.

IGNATIUS OF LOYOLA